A+ books

Bilingual Picture Dictionaries

My First Book of Italian Words

by Katy R. Kudela

Translator: Translations.com

apple
la mela
(MAY-lah)

CAPSTONE PRESS
a capstone imprint

Printed and bound in the USA.

Table of Contents

Printed and bound in the USA. PO#

How to Use This Dictionary

This book is full of useful words in both Italian and English. The English word appears first, followed by the Italian word. Look below each Italian word for help to sound it out. Try reading the words aloud.

Topic Heading in English

Topic Heading in Italian

Word in English
Word in Italian
(pronunciation)

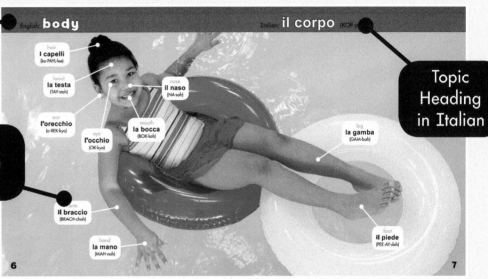

English **body**   Italian **il corpo** (KOR-poh)

hair
i capelli
(ka-PAYL-lee)

head
la testa
(TAY-stah)

nose
il naso
(NA-soh)

ear
l'orecchio
(o-REK-kyo)

mouth
la bocca
(BOK-kah)

eye
l'occhio
(OK-kyo)

leg
la gamba
(GAM-bah)

arm
il braccio
(BRACH-choh)

hand
la mano
(MAH-noh)

foot
il piede
(PEE-AY-deh)

6   7

Notes about the Italian Language

The Italian alphabet has 21 letters. The letters "j," "k,", "w," "x," and "y," are not used. They do appear in foreign words, such as "jeans."

The Italian language usually includes "il," "i," "la," "lo," and "l" before nouns. These all mean "the" in Italian. The pronunciations for these articles are below.
il (eel)   i (ee)   la (lah)
lo (loh)   l' (l)

uncle
lo zio
(ZEE-oh)

cousin
il cugino
(ku-JEE-noh)

mother
la mamma
(MAM-mah)

aunt
la zia
(ZEE-ah)

baby
il bebé
(beh-BEH)

4

Italian: la famiglia (fa-MEE-ya)

grandmother
la nonna
(NON-nah)

father
il papà
(pa-PAH)

grandfather
il nonno
(NON-noh)

brother
il fratello
(fra-TAYL-loh)

sister
la sorella
(so-RAYHL-la)

Printed and bound in the USA. P94

hair
i capelli
(ka-PAYL-lee)

head
la testa
(TAY-stah)

nose
il naso
(NA-soh)

ear
l'orecchio
(o-REK-kyo)

mouth
la bocca
(BOK-kah)

eye
l'occhio
(OK-kyo)

arm
il braccio
(BRACH-choh)

hand
la mano
(MAH-noh)

Printed and bound in the USA. PO#

leg
la gamba
(GAM-bah)

foot
il piede
(PEE-AY-deh)

Printed and bound in the USA. PO#

pajamas
il pigiama
(pee-JAH-mah)

coat
il cappotto
(kap-POT-toh)

shorts
i pantaloncini
(pan-ta-lon-CHEE-nee)

boot
lo stivale
(stee-VAH-leh)

shoe
la scarpa
(SKAR-pah)

hat
il cappello
(kap-PAYL-loh)

pants
il pantaloni
(pahn-tah-LOH-nee)

sock
il calzino
(kal-SEE-noh)

dress
il vestito
(vay-STEE-toh)

shirt
la camicia
(ka-MEE-cha)

9

Printed and bound in the USA. PO#

kite
l'aquilone
(a-kwi-LOH-ne)

doll
la bambola
(BAM-boh-lah)

puzzle
i puzzle
(pazl)

train
il treno
(TRE-noh)

wagon
il carro
(KAR-roh)

Printed and bound in the USA.

puppet
la marionetta
(ma-ree-oh-NAYT-tah)

skateboard
lo skateboard
(SKAYEET-bord)

jump rope
la corda per saltare
(KOR-dah PAYR sal-TA-reh)

ball
la palla
(PAL-lah)

bat
la mazza
(MAZ-zah)

window
la finestra
(fee-NAY-strah)

picture
il quadro
(KWA-droh)

lamp
la lampada
(LAHM-pah-dah)

dresser
la cassettiera
(cas-set-TYER-uh)

curtain
la tenda
(TAYN-dah)

blanket
la coperta
(ko-PER-tah)

Italian: la camera da letto (KA-may-rah da LAYT-toh)

door
la porta
(POR-tah)

pillow
il cuscino
(koo-SCHEE-noh)

bed
il letto
(LET-toh)

rug
il tappetino
(tap-peh-TEE-noh)

13

bathtub
la vasca da bagno
(VAH-skah da BAH-nyoh)

soap
il sapone
(sah-POH-neh)

toilet
il gabinetto
(ga-bee-NET-toh)

mirror
lo specchio
(SPEK-kyo)

toothbrush
lo spazzolino da denti
(spaz-zoh-LEE-noh da DAYN-tee)

toothpaste
il dentifricio
(dayn-tee-free-choh)

comb
il pettine
(PET-tee-ne)

sink
il lavandino
(lah-van-DEE-noh)

towel
l'asciugamano
(ah-schoo-gah-MAH-noh)

brush
la spazzola
(SPAZ-zoh-lah)

15

pot
la pentola
(PAYN-toh-lah)

stove
il fornello
(phor-NAYL-loh)

bowl
la scodella
(skoh-DAYL-lah)

oven
il forno
(FOR-noh)

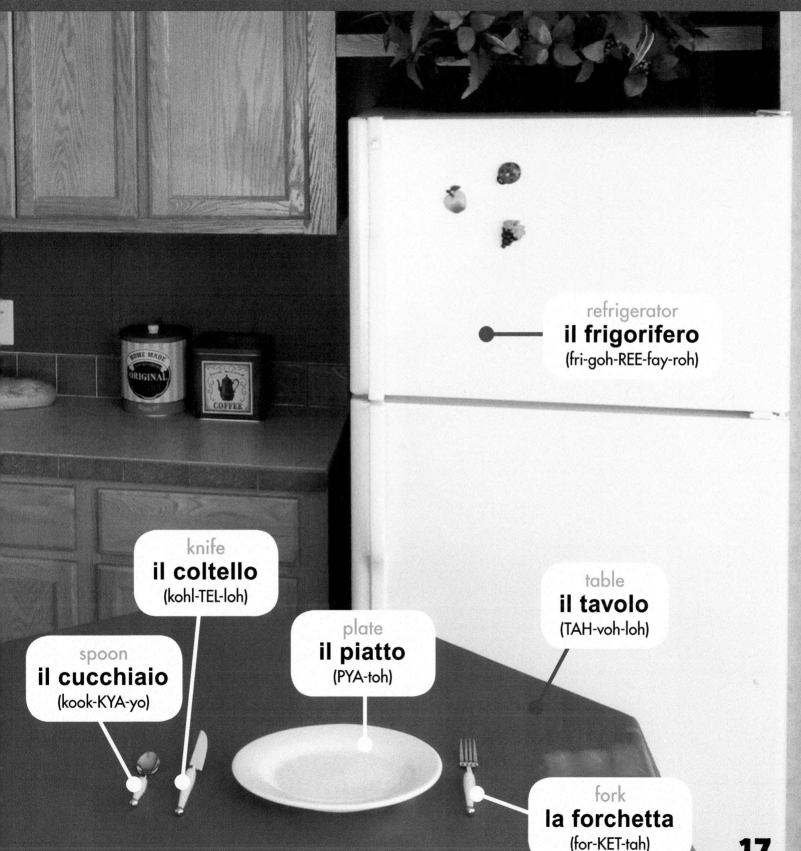

refrigerator
il frigorifero
(fri-goh-REE-fay-roh)

knife
il coltello
(kohl-TEL-loh)

table
il tavolo
(TAH-voh-loh)

plate
il piatto
(PYA-toh)

spoon
il cucchiaio
(kook-KYA-yo)

fork
la forchetta
(for-KET-tah)

17

milk
il latte
(LAT-teh)

carrot
la carota
(ca-RO-tah)

bread
il pane
(PA-neh)

apple
la mela
(MAY-lah)

butter
il burro
(BUR-roh)

Printed and Bound in the USA. 20

Italian: il cibo (CHI-boh)

egg
l'uovo
(WO-voh)

pea
il pisello
(pee-SAYL-loh)

orange
l'arancia
(a-RAN-chah)

sandwich
il panino
(pa-NEE-noh)

rice
il riso
(REE-so)

Printed and bound in the USA. PO#

tractor
il trattore
(trat-TO-reh)

hay
il fieno
(FYE-noh)

fence
il recinto
(re-CHEEN-toh)

farmer
l'agricoltore
(a-gri-kol-TOH-reh)

sheep
la pecora
(PE-koh-rah)

pig
il maiale
(ma-YA-leh)

Printed and bound in the USA.

horse
il cavallo
(ka-VAL-loh)

barn
il fienile
(pheeay-NEE-leh)

cow
la mucca
(MOOK-kah)

chicken
il pollo
(POL-lo)

leaf
la foglia
(FO-yah)

butterfly
la farfalla
(far-FAL-lah)

flower
il fiore
(FYO-reh)

shovel
la pala
(PAH-lah)

bird
l'uccello
(ooc-CHEL-loh)

worm
il verme
(VAYR-meh)

Printed and bound in the United States

plant
la pianta
(PYA-ntah)

grass
l'erba
(AYR-bah)

dirt
il terreno
(ter-REH-noh)

seed
il seme
(SAY-meh)

23

purple
il viola
(vee-OH-lah)

brown
il marrone
(mahr-RO-neh)

orange
l'arancione
(a-ran-CHO-ne)

white
il bianco
(BYAN-koh)

red
il rosso
(ROS-soh)

black
il nero
(NAY-ro)

pink
il rosa
(RO-sa)

blue
il blu
(bloo)

yellow
il giallo
(JAL-loh)

green
il verde
(VAYR-de)

25

in the USA. PO#

teacher
insegnante
(en-say-NYAN-teh)

book
il libro
(LEE-broh)

desk
la cattedra
(KAT-tay-drah)

pencil
la matita
(ma-TEE-tah)

crayon
il pastello
(pa-STAYL-loh)

Printed and bound in the USA. PO#

map
la mappa
(MAHP-pah)

clock
l'orologio
(oh-roh-LO-joh)

computer
il computer
(kohm-PYOO-ter)

chair
la sedia
(SAY-dya)

paper
la carta
(KAR-tah)

27

traffic light
il semaforo
(se-MA-fo-ro)

library
la biblioteca
(bib-lee-oh-TAY-kuh)

store
il negozio
(nay-GO-zee-oh)

LIBRARY

ONE WAY

Tuesday 2:00-5:00
Thursday 2:00-6:00

bicycle
la bicicletta
(bee-chee-KLAYT-tah)

car
l'automobile
(ahoo-to-MO-bee-le)

Printed and bound in the USA. PO#

tree
l'albero
(AL-bay-roh)

bus
l'autobus
(AHOO-to-boos)

park
il parco
(PAR-ko)

street
la via
(vee-a)

sign
il cartello stradale
(car-TEL-loh strah-DAHL-lay)

STOP

29

Printed and bound in the USA. PO#

Numbers • Numeri (NOO-may-ree)

1. one • **uno** (OO-noh)
2. two • **due** (DOO-ay)
3. three • **tre** (tray)
4. four • **quattro** (KUAT-troh)
5. five • **cinque** (CHIN-kwe)

6. six • **sei** (SAY)
7. seven • **sette** (SAYT-teh)
8. eight • **otto** (OT-toh)
9. nine • **nove** (NOH-veh)
10. ten • **dieci** (DYE-chee)

Useful Phrases • Frasi utili (frah-see oo-tee-lee)

yes • **sì** (see)

no • **no** (noh)

hello • **ciao** (CHOW)

good-bye • **arrivederci** (ar-ree-vay-DAYR-chee)

good morning • **buon giorno** (bwon JOR-noh)

good night • **buona notte** (bwo-nah NOHT-teh)

please • **per favore** (PAYR fah-VOH-reh)

thank you • **grazie** (GRAY-zeeay)

excuse me • **scusa** (SCOO-sah)

My name is _____. • **Il mio nome è _____.** (eel MEE-oh NOH-meh AY)

Printed and bound in the USA. PO#

Read More

Let's Learn Italian Picture Dictionary. Passport Books New York: McGraw-Hill, 2002.

Turhan, Sedat. *Milet Mini Picture Dictionary: English-Italian.* London: Milet Publishing, 2003.

Internet Sites

FactHound offers a safe, fun way to find Internet sites related to this book. All of the sites on FactHound have been researched by our staff.

Here's all you do:

Visit www.facthound.com

Type in this code: 9781429652650

 Check out projects, games and lots more at
www.capstonekids.com

A+ Books are published by Capstone Press,
1710 Roe Crest Drive, North Mankato, Minnesota 56003.
www.capstonepub.com

Library of Congress Cataloging-in-Publication Data
Kudela, Katy R.
  My first book of Italian words / by Katy R. Kudela.
    p. cm. — (A+ Books, Bilingual picture dictionaries)
  Includes bibliographical references.
  Summary: "Simple text paired with themed photos invite the reader to learn to speak Italian"—
Provided by publisher.
  ISBN 978-1-4296-5265-0 (library binding)
  ISBN 978-1-4296-6159-1 (paperback)
  1. Picture dictionaries, Italian. 2. Picture dictionaries, English. 3. Italian language—Dictionaries,
Juvenile—English. 4. English language—Dictionaries, Juvenile—Italian. I. Title. II. Series.
PC1629.K83 2010
453'.21—dc22   2010029470

Credits
Lori Bye, designer; Wanda Winch, media researcher; Eric Manske, production specialist

Photo Credits
Capstone Studio/Gary Sundermeyer, cover (pig), 20 (farmer with tractor, pig)
Capstone Studio/Karon Dubke, cover (ball, sock), 1, 3, 4–5, 6–7, 8–9, 10–11,
    12–13, 14–15, 16–17, 18–19, 22–23, 24–25, 26–27
Image Farm, back cover, 1, 2, 31, 32 (design elements)
iStockphoto/Andrew Gentry, 28 (main street)
Photodisc, cover (flower)
Shutterstock/Adrian Matthiassen, cover (butterfly); David Hughes, 20 (hay); Eric Isselee,
    20–21 (horse); hamurishi, 28 (bike); Ievgeniia Tikhonova, 21 (chickens); Jim Mills, 29
    (stop sign); Kelli Westfal, 28 (traffic light); Margo Harrison, 20 (sheep); MaxPhoto, 21
    (cow and calf); Melinda Fawver, 29 (bus); Robert Elias, 20–21 (barn, fence); Vladimir
    Mucibabic, 28–29 (city skyline)

Note to Parents, Teachers, and Librarians
Learning to speak a second language at a young age has been shown to improve overall
academic performance, boost problem-solving ability, and foster an appreciation for other
cultures. Early exposure to language skills provides a strong foundation for other subject
areas, including math and reasoning. Introducing children to a second language can help
to lay the groundwork for future academic success and cultural awareness.

Printed and Printed in the United States   4078